IN THE
NATIONAL INTEREST

General Sir John Monash once exhorted a graduating class to 'equip yourself for life, not solely for your own benefit but for the benefit of the whole community'. At the university established in his name, we repeat this statement to our own graduating classes, to acknowledge how important it is that common or public good flows from education.

Universities spread and build on the knowledge they acquire through scholarship in many ways, well beyond the transmission of this learning through their education. It is a necessary part of a university's role to debate its findings, not only with other researchers and scholars, but also with the broader community in which it resides.

Publishing for the benefit of society is an important part of a university's commitment to free intellectual inquiry. A university provides civil space for such inquiry by its scholars, as well as for investigations by public intellectuals and expert practitioners.

This series, In the National Interest, embodies Monash University's mission to extend knowledge and encourage informed debate about matters of great significance to Australia's future.

Professor Margaret Gardner AC
President and Vice-Chancellor,
Monash University

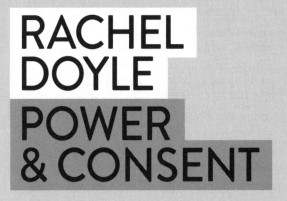

RACHEL DOYLE
POWER & CONSENT

MONASH
UNIVERSITY
PUBLISHING

Power & Consent
© Copyright 2021 Rachel Doyle
All rights reserved. Apart from any uses permitted by Australia's *Copyright Act 1968*, no part of this book may be reproduced by any process without prior written permission from the copyright owners. Inquiries should be directed to the publisher.

Monash University Publishing
Matheson Library Annexe
40 Exhibition Walk
Monash University
Clayton, Victoria 3800, Australia
https://publishing.monash.edu

Monash University Publishing brings to the world publications which advance the best traditions of humane and enlightened thought.

ISBN: 9781922464125 (paperback)
ISBN: 9781922464149 (ebook)

Series: In the National Interest
Editor: Louise Adler
Project manager & copyeditor: Paul Smitz
Designer: Peter Long
Typesetter: Cannon Typesetting
Proofreader: Gillian Armitage
Printed in Australia by Ligare Book Printers

A catalogue record for this book is available from the National Library of Australia.

The paper this book is printed on is in accordance with the standards of the Forest Stewardship Council®. The FSC® promotes environmentally responsible, socially beneficial and economically viable management of the world's forests.

AUTHOR'S NOTE

In this book, for the sake of convenience, I refer to the provisions of the *Sex Discrimination Act 1984* (Commonwealth). The provisions in the cognate state Acts which prohibit sexual harassment are relevantly the same.[1]

For the sake of brevity, I use the terms perpetrator / sexual harasser and victim / complainant. Of course, I accept that the fact that allegations of sexual harassment have been made does not constitute proof of the same.

Again, for brevity, I generally refer to complainants as 'she' and perpetrators as 'he'. This is not intended to ignore or diminish the experiences of men who are victims of sexual harassment, nor is it intended to suggest that women do not ever perpetrate sexual harassment.

Thank you to James Ryan, barrister, for proofreading and research assistance. Thanks also to Paul Smitz for the editing, and Louise Adler for encouraging this work.

POWER & CONSENT

On the morning of 22 June 2020, a friend texted me two words: *pretty explosive*. Below his message was a link to an online newspaper article. This was my introduction to a story which would ignite vigorous debate within the legal profession and the wider community for months to come.

I clicked through. The Chief Justice of the High Court of Australia, Susan Kiefel, had just issued a statement. In a few terse paragraphs, an unprecedented era of soul-searching by the legal profession was ushered in, beginning with: 'The High Court was advised last year of allegations of sexual harassment against a former Justice and we immediately acted to commission an independent investigation.' The investigation had taken some months to complete, and the statement went on to confirm that its subject was the Hon Dyson Heydon AC QC. The inquiry had found that 'six former Court staff members who were Judges' Associates were harassed by the former Justice'.

Six! Six former associates to judges of the High Court of Australia had been found to have been harassed by a High Court judge! The Chief Justice's statement continued:

> The findings are of extreme concern to me, my fellow Justices, our Chief Executive and the staff of the Court. We're ashamed that this could have happened at the High Court of Australia.
>
> We have made a sincere apology to the six women whose complaints were borne out. We know it would have been difficult to come forward. Their accounts of their experiences at the time have been believed. I have appreciated the opportunity to talk with a number of the women about their experiences and to apologise to them in person.[2]

I am familiar with this economical judicial style of writing. I've been a barrister for twenty-five years. I was an associate to a High Court judge from 1994 to 1995. I know the style deployed by some judges. Not one word is wasted; every phrase is infused with meaning.

I was rocked by the Chief Justice's use of the phrase 'We're ashamed'. The pronoun 'we', and the ownership that conveys. Then there was the reference to shame, a feeling often provoked in victims of sexual harassment. Yet here was the nation's most senior law officer saying that *she* felt shame because of what had happened at her court.

Then there was this: 'We have made a sincere apology ...' Which, it is revealed later in the same passage, was (at least with respect to some of the women) an apology delivered to the complainants by the Chief Justice in person.

This was not some disembodied expression of regret from an institution, but a sincere apology from 'me' (the Chief Justice) to the complainants. Her Honour avoided the usual banal expressions of regret doled out by corporations and institutions which tend to imply that the most recent instance of sexual harassment uncovered is the result of some mysterious external force visited upon them, rather than the result of conduct coming from within.

And then the sleeper at the end of that sentence, which described the former associates as the six women 'whose complaints were borne out'. Two sentences later, the statement says: 'Their accounts of their experiences at the time have been believed.' So the Chief Justice was saying to the six women: 'We believe you.'

There were no guarded references to 'allegations' or to 'versions of events' reported to management. No incantation of the refrain that it is not appropriate or possible to offer any commentary on 'the ongoing situation', because the matter is or might be before the courts. Rather, a simple and direct acknowledgment that the accounts of the women 'have been believed'.

The content of the statement was shocking. But a large part of the powerful punch it packed was the language it deployed. Further, it was the Chief Justice who broke the news. She told the world, rather than being pressured into a response to a revelation by someone else. Both in substance and in form, the Chief Justice's statement was an example of how to respond with candour and how to be accountable. She had set the tone, by making it clear that this is not a matter which calls for expressions of mild regret. This is a matter of shame; it requires an apology and calls for changes to be made.

True enough, there may not be another judge or captain of industry in the country who would feel as able as the Chief Justice of the High Court to issue a decree like this one. And true it is, Dyson Heydon immediately denied, and continues to deny, the allegations. But in reflecting upon the statement, it occurred to me that it offers a number of signposts in relation to dealing with sexual harassment in the legal profession, and in workplaces generally.

First, acceptance of the victims' accounts: *We believe you.*

Next, condemnation of the perpetrator's conduct: *This should not have been done to you.*

An apology: *We are sorry.*

Taking responsibility: *We (the institution, the corporation, the profession) are ashamed that this was done to you; we should not have let this happen to you.*

Change: *This will not happen again.*

At first, it seemed shocking that the investigation and its findings concerned six women. But again on reflection, perhaps this was perfectly explicable. No woman had felt able to come forward on her own, as a lone voice. But the six of them had found the courage to act as a group. This prompted many to describe the Heydon case as the law's Me Too moment. Yet there is a crucial difference. The six associates did not go public with their allegations. They did not use social media to drop the story. Rather, they made their complaints to the High Court through a lawyer. They then maintained a careful silence throughout the course of the investigation. Following the investigation, it was the Chief Justice who broke the story.

The methods deployed by the Me Too movement raise some uncomfortable issues for me. My legal training has inculcated in me the need for a strict adherence to the rules of evidence. Those rules mean that in a courtroom, evidence is not rendered more credible by reason merely of there being multiple accounts to the same effect. The tendency evidence rule also provides that evidence of someone's past conduct is rarely admitted into evidence. But the insatiable human appetite for gossip works the other way: if several people say the same thing, it is more likely to be true, and if someone has done something before, he may do it again. The way that we think in the real world is locked in an endless tug of war with my lawyer's brain, which tells me that multiple accounts carry no additional weight, and that propensity reasoning is the refuge of the feeble-minded.

I wondered whether there might be some way in which we could bring our experience of the real world into closer alignment with the rules of evidence.

On the day of the Chief Justice's statement, the president of the New South Wales Bar Association issued a media release which offered this limp addition to the debate: 'Without commenting on the particulars of any individual case, the Bar Association maintains there is no place for sexual harassment in any workplace, including in the legal profession.' In a similar vein, the president of the Victorian Bar wrote to members on 23 June 'in response to the news reported yesterday about sexual harassment perpetrated by one of the leaders of the legal profession'. Both messages condemned sexual harassment and reminded barristers of the existence of complaints procedures and support services for victims. But where was the message designed to disrupt and prevent the behaviour of those who engage in sexual harassment?

By 24 June, I had had an opinion piece published in *The Age*. In it, I called for the associations which regulate the legal profession in Australia to deliver a more direct message to perpetrators. I offered a possible form of words:

> Some of our members still think it is OK to use their power to humiliate more junior practitioners and subject them to uninvited sexual overtures. It's not ok. It contravenes our policies. It is against the law. Stop doing it. If you are having difficulty understanding this bulletin or in refraining from perpetrating sexual harassment, please contact us and we will arrange an intervention to assist you to stop engaging in behaviour which harms our members.[3]

At the end of the article, I directly addressed the perpetrators: 'To the members of the legal profession who persist in perpetrating sexual harassment. Stop it. You ought to be ashamed.'

Almost immediately, my inbox began to fill with messages from barristers, solicitors, judges and legal academics. The emails came from men and women of all ages and levels of seniority within the profession.

The prevailing theme was that the focus needs to be on the perpetrators. Many women wrote that they feel burdened and exhausted by the obligation to monitor and report sexual harassment. They feel crushed by the culture of silence. They just want it to stop.

I am a senior member of a profession whose members are required to uphold the law, yet it is a profession in which sexual harassment continues, despite having been unlawful for over thirty years. Dyson Heydon is not merely some anonymous 'leader of the profession'. The Heydon story was painful confirmation that sexual harassment exists in our profession at the highest level. If we had been kidding ourselves that the intellectual calibre of the appointments to our superior courts would act as a talisman against poor behaviour, then that hope had been dashed. We can no longer pretend this issue is something going on elsewhere, perhaps in small suburban firms where dinosaurs who have not been to the right practice development seminars in the city might still engage in a ribald joke at Friday night drinks. I decided it was time to speak directly to the harassers.

DENIALS

The press reports in June 2020 dutifully reported the only information available from Heydon, which was delivered in the form of an emphatic denial through the firm Speed and Stracey: 'In respect of the confidential inquiry and its subsequent confidential report, any allegation of predatory behaviour or breaches of the law is categorically denied by our client.'

Does the categoric denial mean that the narrative of events supplied by the former associates is denied, or does it rather mean that while the firm's client might accept that certain things happened essentially as the associates described them, he denies that to do so was predatory, or denies that it could have constituted sexual harassment? Could it be argued that for a judge to proposition his associate is not 'predatory', so long as he asks only once, or so long as he asks nicely? Associates are typically young men and women just starting out in the law. They are required to work in close proximity with their judge for a number of months, and then after leaving the role, to continue to work in a profession where he sits at the apex.

During the period he sat on the High Court (2003–13), not only was Heydon one of the seven most powerful lawyers in Australia, he had deep connections at the New South Wales Bar and in academia. His time on the bench was characterised by caustic commentary in judgments and cutting take-downs of his judicial peers. For example, in an article published in 2004, Heydon criticised judicial activism, describing the doctrine of precedent as 'a safeguard against arbitrary, whimsical, capricious, unpredictable and autocratic decisions'.[4] In 2013, Heydon offered his views on judgment writing to ABC Radio, including the observation that a number of his fellow judges 'don't write grammatically'.[5]

In 2018, during an address delivered at the Melbourne Club, Heydon referred to a report on delays in judgment writing and said that judges on the federal and state courts displayed 'a mentality of procrastination', and warned against 'a torpid shared culture of slackness, languor and drift'.[6] A man who so vociferously criticises his peers is hardly someone you want to cross.

SORRY (SEEMS TO BE THE HARDEST WORD)

The second part of the Speed and Stracey press release read: 'Our client says that if any conduct of his has caused offence, that result was inadvertent and unintended, and he apologises for any offence caused. We have asked the High Court to convey that directly to the associate complainants.'

I am very familiar with this sort of non-apology. I have been involved in many conciliation conferences in which litigants have proffered or received apologies in terms as empty as these: 'If I engaged in any conduct which the plaintiff regards as sexual harassment (which I deny), then I am sorry if she experienced any hurt feelings as a result.' This mangled form of words gained a certain vogue in settlements of sexual harassment cases over the last couple of decades.

Over time, I lost faith in the process. I started to head off requests for apologies from complainants, by telling them that there was no point in attempting to extract an apology which would be hedged about with so many caveats as to render it useless, if not insulting. I also generally advise respondents against proffering an apology in such terms, for reasons including that it may serve only to stoke feelings of anger on the other side. These apologies imply that it is the other person's thin skin which is the real problem. They are a tactic designed to subtly redirect attention to the exaggerated emotions of the complainant and absolve the author of any agency.

Next, Speed and Stracey observed on behalf of their client that: 'The inquiry was an internal administrative inquiry and was conducted by a public servant and not by a lawyer, judge or a tribunal member. It was conducted without having statutory powers of investigation and of administering affirmations or oaths.'

Now the complainants were being gaslighted on the basis that the inquiry was conducted by a mere civilian. Some may say this riposte is no more than the result of the muscle memory of a senior jurist, unable to contemplate any way of getting to the truth other than through sworn testimony subjected to the rigours of cross-examination. Others might say it's a wilful misunderstanding of the reality that any internal complaints process initiated by an employer obviously will not involve complainants being cross-examined by counsel for the alleged perpetrator.[7]

IT HAPPENED TO ME

Now, let's get this bit out of the way. I know you want to know whether it has ever happened to me. I was an associate to a High Court judge in the 1990s. I have been in the law for over twenty-five years. You want to know if I was sexually harassed when I was young.

This matters to you, either way. If I have been subjected to sexual harassment, it may serve to explain why I am writing on this topic. I might be damaged, or at the very least invested. On the other hand, if I have never been sexually harassed, it may confirm that I am no more than a meddlesome bystander.

So OK. I will tell you. It has happened to me. A couple of times. I was young and at the beginning of my career. I did not make a formal complaint either time. I did not need to. Let me tell you why.

The first time, I was in my early twenties. The incident occurred after the work Christmas party. It involved an overture, a request to sit on the lap of a male lawyer very senior to me. It was followed by an embarrassing declaration of a desire to kiss me, which I repelled. The incident was confusing and upsetting.

An apology was delivered in person, the morning after the event. He came to the door of my office and said he had thought about his behaviour the previous night, realised he had done the wrong thing, and wanted to say he was embarrassed and sorry.

On the second occasion, I was about thirty, and a junior barrister. The incident occurred early one evening, in a lift in the barristers' chambers. I was leaving a function. He had either been at the same function or perhaps had been drinking elsewhere in the building. We were the only two in the lift. He stood very close to me, backing me against the wall, and got right in my face, so near that I could smell the booze. He said, 'Look at you! I like your skin, I'd love to touch it, so soft.' The lift doors opened. He stepped out before me; I stayed back. As he lumbered off down the hallway, I stayed in the lift and yelled at his back, 'I will call the Women Barristers Association about this tomorrow. You are a dead man!' He did not turn around. He picked up his pace slightly and ambled out of my sight.

The next day I was contacted by a colleague, also a very senior male barrister. He said the man from the lift the previous evening had rung him. The intermediary had been asked to call me to see if I would be willing to meet so that the man could apologise to me personally, and failing that, he wanted to offer his apology through the intermediary.

What is striking about my experience is that on both occasions, the perpetrator sought me out, and within thirty-six hours had offered an apology. I did not ever have to complain to them or about them. I did not have to tell anyone what had happened, much less repeat my story or submit to cross-examination. In both cases, I received an apology which did not attempt to diminish the conduct, nor question my role in the events or seek to attribute blame elsewhere.

Crucially, I experienced no ramifications in relation to my work or professional life. Indeed, in the first case, on receipt of the apology, I extracted a commitment from *him*. As he stood shifting on his feet in my doorway, I said I accepted his apology, but I had one thing I needed him to promise: that he would not, out of embarrassment, cease assigning good cases to me which required working closely with him. He agreed. He stuck to that agreement.

With respect to the man in the lift, although I declined the offer to meet in person, I asked the intermediary to take this message back to his friend: 'This is my workplace. This is where I earn my income. I have a right to travel in the lift without being harassed. Don't do it again.' He didn't. At least not to me.

I am lucky. I am also no fool. I know why both these events ended so well for me. I am confident, with an emphatic way of expressing myself. I also come from a legal family, and both men knew that.

I know these two things are relevant to the story. In fact, perhaps they are the story—they explain why I felt I could speak so directly to both of them, and probably why they came to apologise.

Each of the events I have just described could have gone another way. I may have been left to agonise over who to tell, when and how. I may have been forced to give my account, repeat it, had it questioned and debated. I might have made a complaint years later, and been criticised for waiting so long. When faced with a formal process and public opprobrium, the men might have denied it. My account would likely have been prodded and tested. I might have been asked what was I doing at the party, how much had I drunk, why was I at the lift at that time, where had I been, why did I step into the lift when a man was already inside it. Why hadn't I told anyone about this before? Why did I wait so long? Such an experience may have caused me to doubt myself, to lose faith in the process, to lose patience, to lose time, to lose my mental health. Instead, I received an apology almost immediately, a promise it would not happen again, and my work life did not change.

I've barely thought about either event since. I have not had to. Both men released me immediately from the burden of carrying the incident alone. They made the episode their problem, their burden. Almost as soon as I registered the insult, I was made whole again by sincerely expressed apologies. I was heard. I felt seen.

I have to wonder, though, if had not possessed the confidence which comes from having grown up in the law, would things have gone the same way? I doubt it.

So I know I am lucky. Probably uniquely so. As a result, my story perhaps offers no example for anyone else because of its singularity.

Or can we wrestle something of greater value from my experience? If anything, perhaps this. I see these features in my story: a rapid acceptance of blame, delivery of a genuine apology, and being relieved of the embarrassment of having my complaint held up for examination by others. Surely these are among the reasons why I was not harmed by these events, and why I was able to move on? Others have not been so lucky. This book is for them. But more importantly, it is also addressed to the men who still do not get it.

A NEW APPROACH

The Australian Human Rights Commission's (AHRC) 2020 *Respect@Work* report calls the current legal and regulatory system 'simply no longer fit for purpose'. The report proposes a new model which needs to be 'evidence-based, victim-focused and framed through a gender and intersectional lens.'[8]

This all sounds very important. But it also leaves me a bit cold. I know that the desire to be *victim-focused* comes from a good place, but I can't help wondering why the response ought not be *perpetrator-focused*. Surely we want to stop them doing what they do? Isn't that more important? Or, at least, doesn't that come first?

But the reports routinely published in relation to sexual harassment are not written for or to the perpetrators. The reports do not offer them any instruction on how to stop harassing. To be frank, these reports are barely even *about* the perpetrators. Perpetrators remain, for the most part, in the shadows. When reading these august reports, you could be forgiven for thinking that the propensity to indulge in sexual harassment is no more than a condition which indiscriminately afflicts some unfortunate men, rather than something within their control to stop.

All the surveys and reports I read suffer from the same problem: they preach to the converted, they generate earnest seminars which are attended by good men and women who nod their heads during the lesson before adjourning to the foyer for mineral water and canapes ... but those people are not the ones who need training in how not to sexually harass. The harassers aren't at the seminars.

We also need to move away from the current reactive model which places a burden on individual complainants to prosecute their complaint.

I have spent a lot of time thinking about a new way to confront this problem. I offer these ideas.

First, we must stop the conduct. The existing legislation and policies require perpetrators to operate with sophisticated levels of empathy and skills of perspective-taking which they clearly do not possess. It may be too late to throw out the clunky definition of sexual harassment in the legislation, but it is not too late to overhaul the way we explain what is welcome conduct and what is not, and it is not too late to teach a new way of talking about consent.

Next, we must break down the culture of silence. This will need us to increase the level of reporting of sexual harassment, including by empowering complainants to act together against recidivist sexual harassers. We need a safe and fair means for victims of the same harasser to identify each other, and we need a way for them to complain together which is more sophisticated and nuanced than the blunt tool of social media campaigns.

We also ought to cultivate policies which require managers and co-workers to call out sexual harassment and be brave enough to confront harassers on the spot. But in addition, we must make a controversial change. Those in managerial positions and senior members of professions ought to be required to report occurrences of sexual harassment which they witness, or which are brought to their attention.

We ought to discourage confidential settlements of sexual harassment complaints other than in limited circumstances. Whenever possible, the details of sexual harassment complaints which are found proven ought to be communicated within the workplace in which they occur. This will encourage more frank discussion about sexual harassment, and it has greater deterrent value.

We also need to change the way complaints of sexual harassment are responded to in workplaces. We need to stop insisting upon processes which mimic litigation and judicial inquiries. Here, we have to find a sensible middle ground between the unmediated chaos of Me Too and the employment security and rights of procedural fairness owed to those accused of sexual harassment.

Finally, we must make proof of allegations against recidivist sexual harassers easier. This will require a change to the way the courts apply the tendency rule of evidence in civil litigation.

1969: PROOF

In mid-2019, I travelled to Oxford with my four siblings to surprise my parents, who were celebrating their fiftieth wedding anniversary. They had been married at Magdalen College chapel in 1969 while my father (a Rhodes scholar) was studying. As part of the anniversary celebrations, there was a small catholic ceremony planned at the chapel, during which my parents would renew their vows.

One of my sisters had compiled a scrapbook of photos and memorabilia from the original service. I pored over the black and white photos of the wedding and the afterparty. For reasons my parents have never satisfactorily explained, the only photos we have (other than one or two of the married couple coming out of the chapel) are the photographer's proofs, which means although beautifully shot and developed in moody sepia tones, each photo has the watermark

'PROOF' embossed on it, the word appearing as raised text which looks as if it has been burnt or branded into the photo.

The photographer took a number of lovely informal shots of the party. Overseas students, mostly from Commonwealth countries, mingled, cradling tumblers. Some of the women (including my maternal grandmother, on her first and only overseas trip) wore hats. The men sported thin ties. The guests in the photos radiate intelligence and scholarly earnestness.

Something about one of the photos caught my eye the first time I flicked through the digital album on my phone. This photo was of a group of three men. Unlike the other guests, their faces are serious. They could just as easily be at a funeral as a wedding. Their suits are dark, and the mood sombre, almost tense. The two men closest to the photographer are looking at each other, across the camera's gaze; it appears as if the man on the right has just made a weighty point. The third man is not making eye contact with either of the others. His body is facing the photographer, but his eyes under thick black horn-rimmed glasses are looking off to the side. He is biting his bottom lip. He looks uneasy, or possibly embarrassed. I wondered who this stern man was, looking askance. I held up the photo on my phone and showed my parents. 'Oh, that's Dyson Heydon,' one of them said. 'I'd forgotten he was at our wedding.' It turns out Heydon was at Oxford at the time, having stayed on to teach after completing his own studies as a Rhodes scholar.[9]

This meant little to me at the time. This was months before the scandal that would break in the first half of 2020. Of course I knew who Heydon was. I'd read his judgments. I had also appeared briefly for the Plumbers Union in 2014 during the Royal Commission into Trade Union Governance and Corruption, over which he presided. But in mid-2019, on holidays, when I first came across this photo, his presence at the wedding was of no more than idle interest.

More recently, I went back to the online repository of my parents' anniversary album, searching for that photo. It registered differently this time. Knowing it was Heydon, yes, but more importantly, also knowing *where* he was, both literally and in terms of the trajectory of his glittering legal career. He was at Oxford, at the beginning of it all. The photo was taken prior to his appointment as dean of Sydney University Law School, before his career at the New South Wales Bar, his elevation to the New South Wales Court of Appeal, his appointment to the High Court, his return to Oxford after the court, the trade union royal commission and … the revelations of 2020.

Revisiting that photo, I looked again at this man who was in a group but not part of the conversation, looking somewhere else. I wondered what or who Heydon was looking at beyond the camera. I wondered whether he spoke to any women at the party. I wondered what was in the tumbler he was holding. Now I was looking at a photo of a man all of Australia was talking about. A photo of a man standing below a sign which read: 'PROOF'.

IS THERE A PROBLEM?

The legal position is clear. In Australia, sexual harassment in the workplace has been unlawful for decades. Some states introduced anti-discrimination legislation in the late 1970s; the *Sex Discrimination Act* (Cth) commenced operation in 1984.

There is no need for me to pen yet another piece on the prevalence of sexual harassment in the workplace or in the legal profession. Others have done this essential work. I have read so many reports about sexual harassment. They are generally well researched and well written. There's so much earnest thinking and writing on this topic. So much data. So much analysis. So little change.

The reports tell us there is a problem with sexual harassment, and there has been for years. The reports tell managers there is good reason to be concerned, and counsel them to ensure they run training programs, establish complaints procedures and keep data about progress. These statistics are unassailable, and the rates of harassment and the level of non-reporting have remained stubbornly around the same level for some time, in both workplaces generally and in the legal sector in particular.

Since 2003, the AHRC has conducted four periodic surveys on the national experience of sexual harassment. Its 2018 survey *Everyone's Business: Fourth National Survey on Sexual Harassment in Australian Workplaces* confirmed that sexual harassment in Australian workplaces was widespread: one in three people had experienced sexual harassment at work in the previous five years (39 per cent of women and 26 per cent of men).[10] Four out of five of those harassed were sexually harassed by a male.[11] The majority of workplace sexual harassment took place within Australia's four largest industries.[12]

The AHRC's *Respect@Work* report, which runs to over 900 pages, followed an inquiry which ran for over a year. The commission bleakly noted that in over thirty-five years, the rate of change had been disappointingly slow, and Australia now lags behind other countries in preventing and responding to sexual harassment.[13] The situation in the legal profession is no better; on the whole, it's worse. Recent reports have confirmed that over 30 per cent of women in the

Australian legal profession have experienced sexual harassment at work.[14]

Who are the sexual harassers? Big reveal: most harassers are male.[15] Beyond this, it is difficult to identify any typical characteristics of a person who engages in sexual harassment. They are to be found in all age groups, industries and social backgrounds.

The AHRC survey provided some additional insights. Of the respondents who had been sexually harassed in the preceding five years, 79 per cent said that one or more of their harassers was male.[16] Where the most recent incident involved a single harasser, more than half (54 per cent) indicated that the harasser was aged forty or older.[17]

And of course, harassers often strike again. The survey found that 41 per cent of those who said they had been sexually harassed in the workplace in the last five years were aware that others in their workplace had experienced sexual harassment, most often at the hands of the same harasser.[18] This data confirms that one of the big problems any attempt to tackle harassment must face is the phenomenon of recidivists.

But why do they do it? My initial glib response to this question was: because they can. Following lengthy and mature reflection, I can now confirm that the answer is: *because they can*.

Power is important. The law is a hierarchical profession. There are clearly designated ranks: clerk, graduate, lawyer, associate, senior associate, partner. Barristers progress through the roles of reader, junior counsel and senior counsel—and perhaps ultimately, judge. A reasonable period of time is required to be served at each stage (and high proficiency generally required to be displayed) in order to move to the next level. As a result, in the law, age is a good proxy for seniority and status. It is not determinative—for example, I have had junior counsel working with me who are older than I. But it is fair to say that in the law, age is a fair proxy for one's position in the hierarchy. The power dynamic is overt. The partner of the firm who will determine whether you get a promotion or a pay increase wields power over you every day. It is obvious to junior barristers that senior counsel possess the power to affect their reputation and flow of work at the Bar.

It is very likely that this power structure has contributed to a culture of silence in the law. The same can no doubt be said of medicine, the military and many other fields where the hierarchy is obvious. But it is also clear that sexual harassment is not confined to situations where a harasser is in a position of explicit seniority over the victim. The AHRC report found that the most common relationship between harassers was a co-worker employed at the same level (27 per cent for single harassers and 35 per cent for multiple harassers).[19]

Feminist scholars argue that gender inequality in society helps to explain the prevalence of sexual harassment in circumstances where the imbalance in power between the harasser and victim does not fit a commonly recognised pattern, like a disparity in age, seniority or authority. Understood this way, sexual harassment by men perpetrated against women who are their peers is the manifestation of an attempt to gain power over them. The feminist analysis is that the maintenance of an atmosphere in workplaces which routinely devalues women's contributions, and in which they are sexualised and degraded, serves to undermine all women, and to reduce their potential advancement.[20] Shi and Zhong argue that the conception of sexual harassment as individualised, aberrant behaviour entirely fails to address these broader structural and systemic issues.[21]

Women in powerful positions are sometimes harassed by men who hold *less-powerful* positions. This 'harassing up' is often in the nature of derogatory gender-based comments or sexist jokes. Again, feminists posit that the harassment in these cases is aimed at undermining women by focusing on stereotypical characteristics attributed to them.[22]

To find out what men say about this, I consulted the website of Male Champions of Change. Yes. That's their name. The Male Champions of Change describe themselves as proponents of a 'disruptive strategy to accelerate the advancement of women in leadership and to achieve gender equality'. You may wonder why it is that a group of men calling upon other men to adhere to existing laws prohibiting discrimination has been awarded the label *champions*. When women talk about sexual harassment, they are humourless feminists. When men form a club to talk about sexual harassment, they award themselves medals for their efforts. Sigh.

In any event, the Male Champions of Change released a report in 2019 in which they proclaimed, from their position on the winners' podium, that 'sexual harassment, in all its forms, is an abuse of power and represents behaviours that are beneath the standard we expect from every one of us and across our organisations'.[23] Here, the Champions nail it. At its core, sexual harassment is indeed an abuse of power. That power usually comes from and is strengthened by a man's position in the workplace hierarchy. But it may also be the personal, not institutional power, which comes simply from being male rather than female. That subtle form of power may derive from working in an environment where no matter how hardworking or intelligent your female co-worker is, she can be brought down instantly by being described or judged by reference to her looks, and where she can, despite her wishes, be talked about, touched and propositioned because she is a woman.

Should we bother to try to fix this? Yes, we must. One does not need to care about the hurt feelings of women or their position in society to know things have to change. Even if you care only about the bottom line, you will want to stamp it out. Sexual harassment represents a cost to Australian employers through lost productivity, sick leave, staff turnover, negative impact on workplace culture, low morale, diversion of resources associated with responding to complaints, litigation and workers' compensation, and reputational damage.[24] A report by Deloitte estimated that, in 2018, workplace sexual harassment cost the Australian economy approximately $2.6 billion in lost productivity and $900 million in other costs.[25]

STOP IT! I DON'T LIKE IT!

We need to teach sexual harassers how to stop. There are lessons to be learned from past interventions in relation to road safety and occupational health and safety. These efforts have involved multi-dimensional campaigns embracing education, advertising, training—and of course, stiff penalties. What those successful campaigns have in common is the use of clear (sometimes confronting) language and images. And their message is aimed at the relevant actor: the dangerous driver, the negligent employer.

If we think about sexual harassment by analogy with road safety, a message like this would not go far: 'If you get hit by a criminally negligent driver who is speeding in proximity to pedestrians, the good news is that we have a system that supports victims to commence litigation against the driver, and to obtain medical treatment and rehabilitation.' How could a message like that motivate negligent drivers to drive more slowly or more safely? No doubt all the PowerPoint presentations given around corporate Australia over the last decade which remind attendees of the available avenues for complaints about sexual harassment have been just as motivating for perpetrators—in short, not at all. Encouraging victims to seek support is nice. But let's tackle the behaviour. That means addressing the perpetrator.

Empathy is pretty fashionable right now. For a while there, I toyed with the idea that empathy training might assist recidivist sexual harassers. Perhaps, I thought, the prevalence of sexual harassment in our society is the result of a widespread failure to be capable of seeing the perspective of the other.

But almost as soon as I set out on the path to learn more about developing empathy muscles, I stumbled. The problem is that a reliance upon empathy to guide one's actions is likely to suffer from being dependent upon finding something in the other which resonates. There is a risk that we find it easier to do things that are beneficial for people like ourselves, but more difficult to do anything for those who are different from us. For this reason, empathy may ultimately only offer the illusion of moral progress, without actually ensuring that anyone does the more difficult work of altering their behaviour.

So I refocused my attention on the conduct we're trying to stamp out. I could not help concluding that it is likely that both the answer and the problem lie in the words of the legislation. Section 28A(1) of the *Sex Discrimination Act 1984* (Cth) provides that sexual harassment is an unwelcome sexual advance, unwelcome request for sexual favours, or other unwelcome conduct of a sexual nature. It now seems clearer to me that the bit that perpetrators struggle with is the 'unwelcome' criterion. Those who harass do not get what this test calls for. Or they do not care.

'Unwelcome' is a subjective test. The word is clunky. It means 'not wanted' or 'uninvited'. So is the problem both as simple and complex as this: would-be harassers should not do things that women in their workplace do not want, but how do you work out what another person wants?

The problem is that section 28A starts off as if it is about to tell the putative sexual harasser something, and then immediately veers off and starts talking about the hurt feelings of the harassed person. The would-be perpetrator looking for guidance has to put themselves in the mind of the other: is the thing I want to do, the thing I'm about to do, unwelcome to her? Is it what she wants?

The uncomfortable truth we now may have to face is that women are well rehearsed in the art of intuiting, reading or predicting what the other person wants. But many men are not. Yet section 28A requires men to do precisely that—divine what the other wants.

It gets more complex. The second limb of section 28A calls upon the would-be perpetrator to figure out whether a reasonable person would have anticipated the possibility that the person harassed would be offended, humiliated or intimidated. Section 28A(2) provides that the circumstances required to be taken into account include the relationship between the person harassed and the harasser. Here we go again. The harasser is required to read minds, or at least possess highly developed skills in empathy.

So often during discussions about these provisions, I hear men genuinely flummoxed by the need to figure out whether a woman wants something or whether she will find something offensive. 'How do you know?' they ask me. They shake their heads, as if they are being asked to translate a magic spell or an impenetrable foreign text. Often, they will also offer up an example of an occasion from their own past in which their romantic interest was initially not reciprocated by a woman to whom they were attracted but later grew into something. This one example will be held up to me as proof of two things: first, it is just not possible to interpret a woman's response; and second—and here's the kicker—sometimes women initially say no, and then later they say yes.

If we know that men find it difficult to intuit what women want in their intimate relationships, why on earth do we think they will know what woman do not want in the workplace?

Then again, the differences between male and female modes of communication may become a convenient crutch in some cases. In 2014, a partner in a law firm was found to have sexually harassed a woman undertaking professional legal training under his supervision. The harassment included repeatedly asking her to have sex with him.[26] In defence of the allegations, it was submitted that the solicitor's conduct towards the trainee was in part the result of him suffering from high-functioning autism. Counsel described his client as 'a man who was obsessed and childlike in his demeanour', and as someone who perceived things 'in his own somewhat limited and at times distorted way'. (It is worth noting that the solicitor was forty-six years old and the principal of his own firm, which he had established over ten years prior to the events in question.)

The complainant, in contrast, was said to be 'a highly functional, articulate, assertive person of about the same age'. While it is correct that the perpetrator and the victim (who came to the law relatively late in life) were about the same age, one can hardly ignore the power disparity between a trainee and the partner who must sign off on her compulsory practical legal training. The tribunal member hearing the case noted dryly that other reports which had been furnished confirmed that the man was seen by his clients, professional colleagues and close friends as a highly competent, respected, intelligent and outgoing solicitor and friend.[27]

These sorts of cases bring to mind the training rolled out in childcare centres around the country over the last few years. Very young children are encouraged to speak directly to playmates (and ultimately adults who may not have their best interests at heart), raising the palm of one hand towards the face of the schoolyard bully and saying emphatically: 'Stop it! I don't like it!' There is no obligation on the child to explain why they don't like it, and the other child must stop what they are doing and say sorry. There is even a song to accompany the campaign:

> When somebody is being mean to you
> When somebody spoils your day
> Maybe this is all you need to do
> This is all you need to say:
> Stop it—I don't like it!

Toddlers all around the country have been empowered by this efficient (and brutal) means of calling out bullies. Of course, it's open to abuse. The toddler might deploy it in order to dodge being called upon to share their blocks. Worse, they might start using it at home to avoid having to eat their greens. And so, I concede there is a risk that if we rolled out a grown-up equivalent, an employee might lean on it in order to avoid performance management or to dodge an inconvenient task. But could a version of it work? To know the answer, we have to respond to the following questions honestly.

Men, are you prepared to accept that if a woman in your workplace responds to a request for a date, a kiss or a naked photo by saying simply, 'Stop it, I don't want this,' you will stop—no angry comeback, no recriminations, no reprisals?

Women, if a male co-worker or supervisor propositions you or makes a lewd remark, are you prepared to be brave and transparent, raise the metaphorical palm of your hand up to his face and say, 'Stop it! I don't like it'?

RED FLAGS

I have also tried to think about these issues by answering the questions male lawyers have asked me: What are the rules? When is it permissible to flirt? Are you trying to legislate fun out of existence?

It is important to make the message clear and accessible and to avoid prudish morality. I am not saying that two people who work together cannot fall in love, cannot date, cannot have a one-night stand. But I do think that there are some metrics which may assist those who have difficulty reading what those around them want and do not want.

Perpetrators—this is for you!

First, get out of your own head. You need to stop thinking about sexual experiences as if they are a game, and as if the women around you (including those in your workplace) are just the field upon which you play. Think about the other person. Really think of them as a person. Exercise your own empathy muscles, or at least try to adopt her perspective. Ask yourself what does *she* want? How do you think she wants this meeting, coffee, lunch, presentation to unfold? Do you honestly believe she wants you to ask her to dinner, touch her leg, snap her bra strap, kiss her cheek, show her a dick pic?

And if your preliminary answer to the above is yes, why do you think that? Now here, be honest with yourself. It is important that you do not make the mistake of assuming you are infinitely interesting and desirable. Remember, if you are senior to her, you may have spent years being in rooms with people who have to show you deference, need your patronage, seek your approval. It is possible that those more junior than you have even on occasion had to pretend to find what you say amusing or interesting. Is there a risk that her smile, her attention, her gaze are affected by a habit or need to seek your approval? Ask yourself if it is possible she is participating in or tolerating this lunch, your bawdy comments, your efforts at flirtation, or enduring your hand on her lower back, because she does not want to upset you or embarrass you by rejecting you. Be honest—is there any chance she has said yes to this drink, or has failed to remove your hand from her back, because it is just so much harder to say no to you than it is to just let it go and pretend everything is OK?

After running through the above primer on 'What does *she* want?', I propose that anyone left in any doubt attempt to apply the following metrics, or 'red flags', in order to ensure you proceed with caution and in accordance with the law.

First, are you older than the woman you are proposing to touch, kiss or proposition? Is that age gap significant, more than ten years? If so, the *first red flag* has gone up!

Second, are you more senior than her? Are you more than one rung higher up in the hierarchy? If so, your *second red flag* has gone up.

Third, ask yourself this question, and answer it honestly: do you hope (or even expect or require) that she will keep what is about to happen secret? If so, this is a huge *third red flag*.

To put it another way: will you be perfectly comfortable if, following this kiss, or lunch or fondle, she tells her mother, best friend, husband—or your colleagues—what has just happened? Or are you expecting (even requiring) her to keep it secret? If you expect secrecy, then this is your *biggest red flag*.

If you get to this point and the red flags of age gap, seniority gap and insistence on secrecy have gone up, then be warned. You are entering high-risk territory. It may be sexual harassment. You need to be careful. You need to do your due diligence. If you genuinely believe that this much younger, more junior woman, who you expect to keep secret what is about to happen, is genuinely interested after applying the metrics I have suggested above, then you may proceed with caution.

The red flag approach may work for people with explicit power over their potential target. But what do we do about those who are about to say something or do something to a co-worker where there is no explicit power disparity?

Well first, I call bullshit on all the whingeing and fretting that taking a harsher stance on sexual harassment in the workplace will serve to cruel the pitch for what would otherwise be beautiful consensual relationships between people who just happened to meet in the office. I accept that many wonderful relationships start at work. But I can tell you that I also feel pretty confident in assuming that not many of those relationships started with a bloke leaning over a woman's desk, taking her notepad and writing on it: 'I just ripped a hole in my jeans ... I don't have underwear on ... I can touch my penis through the hole.'[28] Nor do I think it very likely many great romances kicked off with a man looking at a female employee's chest, making a growling noise, and saying: 'I would like to chew on those.'[29] I also doubt that many romances have been successfully initiated by a man exposing his erect penis in the office.[30]

I gotta ask: are these incidents really the tentative first moves of a great guy who just wants to test out whether someone he's interested in might be willing to go see a movie with him? Are these really examples of a beautiful nascent courtship that humourless feminists are fixated upon wrecking?

Come on. These smutty, demeaning incidents are not the result of some poor novice in love, bumbling his way through and getting it wrong. They are not the work of a misunderstood romantic.

An appeal court had no difficulty dispensing with such arguments advanced by a self-styled Mr Darcy in mid-2020. In *Hughes Lawyers v Hill* [2020] FCAFC 126, it had been found at trial that the supervising partner in a law firm had inundated a junior female solicitor with emails propositioning her and had, on multiple occasions, physically prevented her from leaving her own office unless she gave him a hug. Justice Nye Perram described the emails as 'mawkish and altogether inappropriate'.[31] He went on to say: 'I reject the submission of Senior Counsel for the Appellant that these were the actions of a Mr Darcy. The facts of this case are about as far from a Jane Austen novel as it is possible to be.'[32]

NO TOUCHY / NO ASKY RULE FOR JUDGES

I can't leave this topic without suggesting we should introduce a strict rule for judges. On 26 June 2020, the heads of Australia's Commonwealth courts released a joint statement which said:

> Sexual harassment in any workplace is unlawful and wholly unacceptable. It is also contrary to the demands of justice that judicial officers are sworn to uphold ... For that reason, any form of sexual harassment by a judicial officer is not only reprehensible, but a breach of the public trust.[33]

Surely we can all agree, by reason of the special position occupied by judges in the legal system and the administration of justice, that they simply can't have a sexual relationship with their associates? Judges' associates are usually in their twenties and either fresh out of law school or at a very early point in their career. The age and power imbalance renders the relationship worthy of deep suspicion.

But if the couple's special connection is truly the 'real thing', then surely they can enjoy a wonderful, consensual relationship—once the associate's period of employment ends, usually after a year. While prime minister Turnbull was mocked for his 'no bonking' rule for ministers and their staff, such a rule for the judiciary, in relation to their young associates, is quite different.[34] Judges administer the law; the law prohibits sexual harassment. Why can we not have a no touchy / no asky rule for judges in relation to their associates?

BOMBE ALASKA

The Victorian Bar holds an annual black-tie dinner attended by over 200 barristers and judges. In 2003, when I had been a barrister for about seven years, I attended the dinner. The honoured guests included Chief Justice Murray Gleeson and Justice Heydon of the High Court. A few champagnes in, after the speeches and in the lull before dessert, during which the guests usually left their tables and mingled, I decided it would be a good idea to speak to the chief justice. It wasn't. As I commenced my remarks, I realised I'd had too much to drink. But it was too late to back out. Somehow, and breaking my own land speed record for steering the conversation onto dangerous territory, I found myself demanding that the chief justice tell me how many female associates were presently engaged at the High Court. I asked whether he could assure me that the ratio of women to men had been maintained since 'my day' in the mid-1990s. I can confirm he said, with his customary precision and dryness, that the majority of associates at the court were women.

As we were talking, I became aware of a tall, cadaverous man approaching us from the side. I turned slightly to see Justice Heydon, who'd been sworn in at the High Court a few months earlier. I knew who he was, of course, but had not spoken to him. Chief Justice Gleeson introduced us and said something along the lines of Ms Doyle was just interrogating me about the proportion of female associates at the court. For reasons that are unclear to me now, I launched into an attempt to educate their Honours about the merits of Melbourne's laneways and wine bars, and suggested they try them on the way back to their accommodation.

At that moment, the venue staff began to push past us in order to get to the tables. The dessert that year was the faintly ridiculous selection of bombe alaska. In my memory, the dessert was also flambéed. On reflection, that seems unlikely. But nevertheless, in my recollection, plates were borne ablaze by staff weaving their way between the mingling guests. One such incendiary device was plonked on a table just to the side of where our uncomfortable group was positioned. I recall that Justice Heydon eyed the dessert with what might have been glee, or with what equally might have been horror—his Coke bottle spectacles made it hard to know. 'You should have some,' I said uncertainly, 'if you want.' I was growing less sure of my role in this trio with every passing second. I stared at the plate of scorched meringue, now listing to one side.

Fear not. The night did not end with me walking with Justice Heydon back to his accommodation via the cobbled laneways of Melbourne. I have nothing further to report.

Except that it now occurs to me that just as was the case at my parents' wedding party in 1969, Dyson Heydon had just joined two other people at a function who were having their own conversation. He was there, but he was not really part of it. He was looking elsewhere; his eye had been caught by something shinier and sweeter. But in our strange trio there was also present a man who was undoubtedly more powerful and important than he. And that man, as he is wont to do, decided the conversation was over, and it ended.

I left the dinner venue with friends and adjourned to a bar. In 2020, reading the High Court's press release, the night of the 2003 Bar dinner felt more like a bullet dodged.

CULTURE OF SILENCE

The Australian data confirms that fewer than one in five people who are sexually harassed ever make a formal complaint.[35] Two-thirds of those who witness sexual harassment take no action.[36] The main reasons given in Australian studies for not reporting sexual harassment are potential negative impacts on reputation, career and finances; feeling ashamed or embarrassed; and relationships within their community or industry.[37]

Respondents to the Victorian Legal Services Board Commissioner Report 2019 gave as the most common reason for not reporting sexual harassment, a desire to avoid confronting the harasser (70 per cent).[38]

The International Bar Association (IBA) reported in 2019 that three-quarters of those who experience sexual harassment do not report the incident.[39] The main reason given for not reporting was the profile or status of the perpetrator, followed by concerns about repercussions.[40]

Further, even after a victim of sexual harassment reaches a resolution of her claim, whether in the context of a settlement of litigation or otherwise, it is routine for the terms of settlement to be confidential. It is also typical for such agreements to include 'non-disparagement clauses' which may prevent a complainant from discussing her grievance with work colleagues or anyone else.

The debate about non-disclosure agreements and confidential settlements is complex. The original rationale was to promote generous settlements by acting as an incentive to harassers and their employers to resolve the matter without recourse to litigation, with all the uncertainty, cost and delay that entails.[41] On the other hand, the primary use of confidentiality agreements is undoubtedly to protect the reputation of the business or the harasser.[42] Put crudely, employers may use non-disclosure clauses to buy silence and protect reputations.[43] This is especially true of cases involving the most serious harassment. Those employers have an incentive to settle the most serious claims, in order to avoid high damages and negative publicity.[44] The phenomenon of victims leaving the workplace with a confidential settlement payment, and the perpetrator either remaining in his position or quietly moving to a new workplace, only facilitates 'rolling bad apples'.[45]

The AHRC has expressed concerns about the use of non-disclosure agreements, including their contribution to 'a culture of silence, which disempowers victims, covers up unlawful conduct and facilitates repeat offending'.[46] Confidentiality clauses not only permit perpetrators to conceal and continue patterns of sexual misconduct, they also stymie discussions in the workplace, denying organisations opportunities to educate staff with lessons learned from the process. This severely limits any deterrent effect the process might otherwise have.

One thing is certain: shining a light on more of these stories will assist. If employees know that the way management react to proven allegations of sexual harassment is to support the victim and condemn the harasser, there is greater hope for deterrence, and perhaps a greater potential that other complainants will come forward.[47]

The Law Council of Australia has argued that treating confidentiality solely as a matter of bargaining between two parties ignores both the interests of other parties who might be affected and the broader public interest in the rule of law.[48] I agree. It's clear that confidential settlements of sexual harassment claims are problematic. If they are to persist, then at the very least the terms of the settlement deeds ought to make it explicit that the parties to the agreement are not prevented from reporting crimes to the police, nor from reporting professional misconduct to the regulator.

We could also get more creative. Even where the identities of the parties to the settlement or some of its details are to be maintained as confidential, employers could insist that the basic facts be permitted to be published to the workforce, perhaps in anonymised form, so that the deterrent value of the experience is not lost.

IBA President Horacio Neto points out that legal professionals are required to be of good character. That requirement appears to be at odds with the fact that sexual harassment is widespread in legal workplaces. Neto says we ought address this hypocrisy.[49]

I agree. Rule 42 of the professional conduct rules which apply to Australian lawyers provides that lawyers must not engage in sexual harassment.[50] Lawyers are officers of the court. It is our job to uphold the law. If we are permitted to simply look the other way when it comes to our attention that another lawyer has breached one of our rules of conduct, then we are ignoring our duty to maintain standards in our profession. For this reason, I suggest that consideration ought to be given to changing the professional conduct rules for lawyers to expressly provide that any lawyer who becomes aware that another lawyer has breached the prohibition on sexual harassment in Rule 42 be required to take some action or to inform the regulator.

Those who feel squeamish about this will complain that it requires colleagues to 'dob'. I accept that it also risks removing agency from the victim. But why shouldn't lawyers be required to report those who do not adhere to the rules which govern us all in the practice of our profession? At the very least, I suggest that senior members of our profession who do not call it out or intervene in some way when they see sexual harassment or have it reported to them, are failing to uphold our standards and are ignoring our rules of conduct.

As with lawyers, there is presently no generally applicable positive obligation on managers to report instances of sexual harassment which they witness or which are brought to their attention.[51] In rare instances, employers may insist upon a specific contractual term or require adherence to a code of conduct which specifically requires this, but it is not typical. In my view, until this requirement to report (or at least respond in some way to) instances of sexual harassment is imposed on managers and those in senior positions in their industries and professions, I doubt that we will see much change.

INTERNAL INVESTIGATIONS

It has become common for allegations of sexual harassment in workplaces and institutions to be examined by independent investigators. This approach began as a sensible way of ensuring both that complainants receive a relatively informal and speedy form of redress, and that the alleged harasser is afforded procedural fairness prior to the imposition of any sanction or termination of their employment. But almost as soon as these investigations became common, other problems emerged. Employers required investigators to impose a high standard of proof, because of concerns about potential industrial and legal claims by the alleged perpetrator.[52]

The processes adopted by investigators are routinely attacked in subsequent litigation on the grounds of a failure to afford procedural fairness to the alleged sexual harasser. Litigation is protracted by turgid lines of cross-examination directed at attacking witnesses' credibility based on discrepancies between the account given to the investigator and their evidence in court. To combat these problems, employers started engaging lawyers and retired judges to conduct workplace investigations, presumably in an effort to ensure that the process might be immune from criticism in a subsequent trial. But this in turn contributed to the investigations starting to mimic mini royal commissions, with investigators undertaking increasingly elaborate processes.

As a result, in many instances, these internal investigations have ceased to offer the benefits of a quick and final resolution, and are often no more than the tense first step in what becomes years of disputation.

Sexual harassment investigations conducted in the workplace are not criminal proceedings. Criminal standards of proof are not required, and may in fact be inappropriate.[53] The excessive formality of these internal investigations, and the application of high standards of proof, has no doubt contributed to the under-reporting of sexual harassment.

Of course, any decision to discipline or dismiss an employee for engaging in sexual harassment must be taken in a way that respects their industrial and legal rights. But those rights do not include an entitlement to a personal royal commission and excoriation of the complainant.[54] Subject to the size and nature of a workplace or institution, it should be possible in many instances to adopt less-formal approaches to investigations which are still sufficiently robust. So long as the complainant's account is tested, all direct witnesses are interviewed, and the alleged perpetrator is afforded an opportunity to answer all claims, this ought to suffice.

In addition, for less-serious allegations, there must surely be a legitimate place for calling it out, or the 'tap on the shoulder' by a peer.[55] There are some workplaces and institutions where a low-key meeting between a peer or manager and the perpetrator might serve to educate the alleged harasser and disrupt his conduct, serving to make him realise that he is being 'watched'.

I accept that such strategies are not free from problems and risks.

First, many complainants will not feel comfortable with direct approaches. There is a risk that in any meeting, the alleged perpetrator will respond with a flat denial, or worse, ridicule or venom directed towards the complainant.

Second, there remains a risk that the perpetrator will complain later about a failure to afford procedural fairness. Suppose, for example, that a complainant asks a peer of the perpetrator to address it with him. This is done, and the conversation appears to go well. An apology is conveyed to the complainant and she is pleased. But say the perpetrator strikes again a few weeks later. Now the complainant is very seriously affected and suffers a depressive reaction. In her subsequent claim, she argues that the employer failed to adequately discharge its obligations to her by relying on a casual fireside chat with the perpetrator. Similarly, when the perpetrator's employment is terminated on the basis that he had been warned yet he persisted, he commences his own proceedings, arguing that he was not formally warned and was assured that the chat would not 'go on his record'.

One can see why risk-averse employers continue to lean on the formal investigation as a crutch. But I still think there is a place for less-elaborate investigations and, in relation to some less serious complaints, for the 'tap on the shoulder' approach, rather than a full-blown internal inquiry.

ME TOO

The Me Too movement is about safety in numbers. Where one woman may be too frightened to speak out against a powerful man on her own, if several women simultaneously move against the same man publicly, they may be able to support each other. Of course, it also renders it more likely their accounts will be accepted.

The Me Too movement has brought the issues of sexual assault and harassment out of the shadows, and out of the offices where exit packages are negotiated and signed in secret. It has demonstrated that victims do not have to suffer alone, or in silence. It has helped expose how widespread sexual harassment and sexual assault are. Of course, the statistics were always available in arid reports for anyone who searched them out. But the stories of women have now been afforded a new prominence.

However, Me Too and social media are blunt tools. Often, there is an instantaneous shift from 'allegation' to a settled fact without further testing of the matter. There is a tension between 'calling it out' and a death spiral towards cancel culture, where anonymous, self-righteous internet identities (and, let's face it, equal numbers of internet nobodies) assign themselves the role of accuser, judge, jury and executioner, and who may cause incalculable reputational and commercial harm to someone with a click of the 'send' button, or by pressing 'post'.

Somewhere on the continuum between anonymous denunciation on a social media platform and a gruelling trial in which a victim of sexual harassment is demolished by aggressive cross-examination, must lie a middle ground where a complainant can tell their story honestly and to the best of their ability, where they can be believed and have their story accepted by their employer, educational institution or the professional conduct regulator to whom they complain? Can we find a new approach which does not attempt to mimic a royal commission, and which at the same time would not permit anonymous reports to end someone's career?

There are new technology solutions which may assist. Platforms and smartphone applications are being developed which enable employees to record contemporaneous complaints and supporting evidence in a safe location. Using these tools, the employee can choose to lodge the complaint with management immediately. Or they may select a function which directs the application to search the system for other complaints about the same perpetrator. If they exist, then the reports will be sent to management together.[56]

The attraction of this can be seen immediately. First, the complainant is encouraged to record their complaint contemporaneously, and with some formality, in a secure place. This minimises any later debate about timeliness and accuracy. Second, the complainant who does not feel confident at that time about making a formal complaint on her own, can elect to wait for another time, or ask the system to check whether others have lodged complaints about the same perpetrator. This offers some of the aspects of support and solidarity which are features of Me Too, without the performative aspects of posting accounts to social media. It may assist to identify recidivist perpetrators.

I know it's not perfect. The system could be gamed by a person who lodges a fake, florid account in the hope of flushing out extant complaints against a boss they hate. Or two malcontents could collaborate and lodge false reports which will be matched and sent to management together. But I maintain that these systems are safer and more robust than social media campaigns. They could be particularly useful in large organisations (the public sector, banks, universities, airlines, the army, police forces, hospitals) where multiple complainants in the same workplace or institution would otherwise be unlikely to know of each other's existence. If these systems were able to be shared with regulators, then it would also become possible, for example, to identify lawyers who move from firm to firm—and even to prevent their appointment to the bench!

TRUTH AND ALTERNATIVE FACTS

The first time a client referred to her version of events in relation to an upcoming trial as 'my truth', my skin crawled. Wrong preposition, I thought meanly.

There cannot be *your* truth or *his* truth, I bristled. There is only *the* truth.

After a quarter-century in the law, all I can say is that there may well exist an objective truth. But we have no reliable means of accessing it. In the end, trials are only an expensive version of *she said / he said*.

I have come to understand that most witnesses give testimony which they believe to be honest. Two people can give an honest account of the same event, yet their perspectives are very different because each is indeed telling their truth. In the context of an allegation of sexual harassment, there is also the problem that one woman's humiliation might be a man's innocent light-hearted joke, or one woman's unwelcome sexual overture might be her male co-worker's genuine compliment.

In a 2019 article, Justice Stephen Gageler of the High Court offers some witty reflections on the entry into mainstream usage of the phrase 'alternative facts', in the wake of competing claims concerning numbers of attendees at US president Trump's inauguration. He notes that the essential feature of fact-finding within an adversarial system is that judges and juries are tasked not with the independent pursuit of some ultimate truth, but rather with the arbitration of a contest between parties' competing versions of the truth. Thus, he noted: 'The question for the tribunal of fact is not the abstract question of whether the fact exists but the more concrete question of whether the tribunal is satisfied at the conclusion of the contest that the fact has been proved to the requisite standard.'[57]

He concluded by noting that our system has never 'adopted the illusion that it is involved in an ultimate quest for truth. But nor has it descended to the relativism of countenancing the dispensation of justice as nothing more than the making of an unconstrained choice between the so called alternative facts'.[58]

This must be right: the courts cannot be in the business of simply making an unconstrained choice between competing, alternative facts. But how do we move from competing truths to a version of the truth we can live with?

These concerns have been echoed by Federal Court judges. *Poniatowska v Hickinbotham* [2009] FCA 680 concerned events which occurred in a real estate agency in South Australia. Justice John Mansfield observed:

> Each witness sees events from his or her own perspective. Over time there is sometimes a degree of rationalisation to fit objective material (documents) as it emerges into the understanding of events. Some witnesses' memories become refined by a strong belief in the rightness of their role, so that objectivity is lost to a degree …

There is a tendency in all of us to put past events in a perspective which fits with our own beliefs, but there is an undisputed core of fact underlying many of her allegations ...[59]

His Honour is right: we do tend to put past events in a perspective which 'fits with our own beliefs', but nevertheless there may also exist an undisputed core of fact which underpins the stories we tell.

Ewin v Vergara (No. 3) [2013] FCA 1311 involved very serious allegations that a co-worker had raped a woman after a work function.[60] The two employer entities settled the claims. The trial proceeded against the alleged harasser on his own. He represented himself and cross-examined the complainant. Justice Mordecai Bromberg said:

In searching for the truth, judges are often left to choose between competing and conflicting versions of the same event. This case has been no exception. The determination of this application has required me to choose between diametrically opposite accounts of the same event on countless occasions. I have done so recognising that a witness' preconceptions may influence his or her perceptions of an event ...

A case like this, in which the background facts involve allegations of rape and in which emotions and animosities between the principal protagonists remain raw, provides a context where reconstructed memory faces the most difficult of challenges.[61]

I would also offer this observation: trials are an impossible forum in which to deal with the messiness of truth. The complainant may be exaggerating some details concerning her employment, but she may also be telling the truth about the sexual harassment. There may be an element of reconstruction to her story, but she may also have been assaulted. Some complainants feel the need to cast the harasser as someone whose friendly overtures were always unwelcome and creepy. This compulsion to present a story which is coherent may influence a junior lawyer to omit the fact that initially, she enjoyed working with this partner, and that he complimented her work and supported her in seeking a promotion. The same sorts of pressures might compel an alleged harasser to describe the junior lawyer with whose work ethic he was in fact initially impressed, as always hysterical and prone to exaggeration.

The messy truth is that some complainants are not good at their jobs but have also been sexually harassed.

The even messier truth is that some sexual harassers are intelligent, attractive, socially able and popular at work. But during a hard-fought trial over events which occurred years earlier, it often becomes difficult for both parties, in the glare of the courtroom, to tell a more nuanced story about changing perceptions and feelings over time.

THE TENDENCY RULE

The tendency evidence rule provides that evidence of the character, reputation, conduct or tendencies of a person is not admissible in civil litigation, unless the court is satisfied that the evidence has significant probative value. An even harsher standard applies in criminal cases, where such evidence cannot be used against the accused unless its probative value substantially outweighs any prejudicial effect it may have.[62] These rules are grounded in a deep suspicion of inferential reasoning based on a person's character.

In the real world, we do judge people by their character, for which we treat their previous conduct as a very useful proxy. But judges are required to observe a pious refusal (other than in exceptional circumstances) to permit the inference that because someone has done something in the past, they may be more likely to do something similar in the future.

The High Court has tied itself in knots over the circumstances in which tendency evidence will be permitted to go before a jury. Between 2008 and 2017, the court handed down a number of decisions on the topic. These cases establish that where the prosecution seeks to adduce evidence of sexual conduct by the accused with respect to one victim, this evidence will be admitted where it possesses sufficient probative value. However, where the tendency evidence sought to be adduced relates to multiple complainants, that evidence must possess what the court calls an additional common or 'special' feature before it will be admitted into evidence.[63] But what species of common or special feature is the High Court looking for? It is on this question that the court has, in my view, gotten itself in a terrible tangle.

The subtleties (and difficulties) of the rule were exposed in the 2018 decision of *McPhillamy*.[64] The accused, a priest's assistant, was charged with a sexual assault upon 'A', an eleven-year-old altar boy, in church toilets between 1995 and 1996. The prosecution had sought to put before the jury the evidence of 'B' and 'C', who would testify that in 1985, they had been boarders at a Catholic college where the accused was the assistant housemaster. Their evidence was that when they were aged thirteen, and on occasions when they were homesick, they had gone to the accused's room to seek advice or comfort, and he had sexually abused them. Five High Court judges accepted that the evidence of B and C was capable of establishing that the appellant had an interest in underage boys.[65] But they determined that the evidence did not possess the requisite commonality with the evidence of the assault on A to go before the jury. They said that the supervision exercised by the accused as assistant housemaster in 1985 over vulnerable, homesick boys in his care had little in common with his role as a priest's assistant vis-a-vis an altar boy some ten years later.[66] The conviction was quashed and a new trial ordered.

Come off it. Seriously.

The idea that there exist men with a sexual appetite so specific that it causes them to seek out only boys suffering from the malady of homesickness, and not relatively happy altar boys, or that there exist paedophiles with such a fixed modus operandi that they must prey only upon teenage boys laid low with reactive depression, is hard to accept.

Of course, an outcome like this probably could have been predicted. The court's squeamishness about admitting tendency evidence had been laid bare in two earlier dissenting judgments of justices Gageler and Geoffrey Nettle. In 2017, in the *Hughes* case, Justice Gageler criticised tendency reasoning, saying that it is 'no more sophisticated than: he did it before; he has a propensity to do this sort of thing; the likelihood is that he did it again on the occasion in issue'.[67]

In a similar vein, Justice Nettle worried that an accused charged with stealing might face a prosecution case that he had committed theft against a dozen female victims aged between six and twenty-four, and that those allegations represent such a pattern of interconnected behaviour as to establish a tendency to steal from young female victims.[68]

But with respect, the analogy between sexual assault and theft is wholly inapt for many reasons.

First, a propensity to steal might be the product of a vast range of motives and social influences, including greed, laziness, poverty, drug addiction, antisocial attitudes, or a recidivist streak fuelled by an association with other criminals. But a man's propensity to indecently assault children always requires the existence of an aberrant sexual interest—even accepting that this interest may itself be the product of innumerable social and emotional influences.

Second, for a thief, the identity and attributes of the victim are unlikely to matter much, if at all. On the other hand, to the sexual offender, the attributes of the victim may be important, even critical (including their gender and age).

Finally, sexual behaviour is more complex than theft. Unlike taking things that don't belong to you, sexual conduct (between adults) is sometimes consensual or welcome (and therefore lawful) and sometimes non-consensual or unwelcome (and therefore unlawful, sometimes criminal).

The problem is that the courts assume that there exist readily identifiable categories of sexual predators with particular sexual predilections to which they confine themselves. But how can judges make such pronouncements about sexual preferences unassisted by expert evidence, data or (dare I add) any actual facts from 'the real world'? In my view, it is this sort of musing unassisted by expert opinion which gives rise to unfortunate judicial observations about men with a tendency to assault boys suffering from homesickness, rather than a predilection to prey on resilient altar boys.

In *Hughes*, Justice Gageler acknowledged that 'common experience provides no sure guide' to ascertaining the degree of probability that a man who has sexually assaulted a child in the past will do so again.[69] I agree: it is unsafe and inappropriate for judges to rely on their own experiences, or even what they call 'common experience', to attempt to predict the sexual behaviour of others. But as Cossins notes in a powerful 2018 article, it is not as if this is an area which is devoid of evidence. The literature on child sex offenders confirms that while some make very specific age, gender and relationship choices, many offenders exhibit cross-over behaviour and sexually abuse both boys and girls, or children of different ages. There are many who prey upon both children related to them in some way and those who are not.[70] But these sorts of reports are not commonly referenced by the courts. They apparently prefer to try to work it out for themselves.

The strict limitations placed on the admissibility of tendency evidence are traditionally said to be necessary because of the risk that juries will attach disproportionate weight to such evidence. But this also appears to be no more than an assumption about the way in which juries reason. A 2016 study found 'no support for the long-standing, judicial assumption that jurors in joint trials will engage in impermissible reasoning as a result of the cross-admissibility of dissimilar evidence from two or more complainants.[71] That study involved the recruitment of over a thousand mock jurors who were assigned to ninety mock juries, which deliberated to a verdict after being shown different versions of a video-recorded trial. Contrary to expectations, the study concluded that there was no evidence of emotional or illogical reasoning by juries found in any of the trials involving tendency evidence.

Before I leave the tendency evidence rule, I give you the most curious decision of all: the High Court's

2011 decision in *Stubley*.[72] The appeal related to the criminal trial of a psychiatrist who had been convicted of engaging in sexual activity with two female patients without their consent. The prosecution sought to adduce evidence at trial from two other former patients. No offences had been charged involving those women.

A majority of the High Court (justices William Gummow, Susan Crennan, Kiefel and Virginia Bell) ruled that the evidence from the two patients was inadmissible. The reasoning went like this. Stubley had admitted to having sexual experiences with all four of his former patients. He said he had been an adherent of a school of thought that held that 'sexual relations between doctor and patient was a helpful methodology. He had since come to regard his conduct as ethically unsound and he regretted that it had occurred.'[73] Stubley insisted that the sexual intimacy with all four patients was consensual.[74] The prosecution case was that he had manipulated the two patients whose evidence was sought to be relied on in order to obtain their consent.[75] The court ruled that evidence inadmissible, concluding that:

> Proof of the [defendant's] tendency to engage in
> grave professional misconduct by manipulating his
> younger, vulnerable, female patients into having

sexual contact with him could not rationally affect the likelihood that JG or CL did not consent to sexual contact on any occasion charged in the indictment.

In short, the court said, the prosecution case erroneously conflated 'proof of psychological dominance with proof of absence of consent'.

Wow. Just wow.

Here, the High Court is saying that an admission that a psychiatrist had, over a number of years, engaged in sex with two female patients could not go before the jury considering charges of sexual assault against two other patients, because those were occasions on which the psychiatrist used his dominant position to *obtain* consent, rather than situations in which he proceeded to have sex *without* consent. So the four events were not similar enough to go before a jury.

Justice Heydon disagreed. Typically, his dissent was blistering.[76] In a key passage, his Honour articulated (albeit in dry legal language) what we all know to be true—there is strength in numbers. I will let Heydon's words speak for themselves on this topic:

[T]o many people ... an allegation that a psychiatrist was engaging in sexual intercourse with a female patient suffering from a mental disturbance which it was his duty to treat would seem so serious and inherently unlikely as to be startling, outlandish and far-fetched to the point of being bizarre. It would seem so bizarre, in the absence of corroboration, that it would be extremely difficult for the prosecution, in a case of oath against oath about conduct taking place in secret, to exclude a reasonable doubt. Thus a prosecution which rested on a single allegation by JG might very easily founder, however truthful she was. A prosecution including all JG's allegations might also easily founder: it would be easy for the defence to rely on her mental illness, her delay in complaint, the long lapse of time and so forth. A prosecution in which CL's evidence was admissible on each count concerning JG and vice versa—a state of affairs the validity of which the accused at no stage, in no court, challenged—would be a prosecution supported by evidence of much greater probative value. And a prosecution supported by the evidence of three other women giving similar testimony about the tendency of the accused to engage in acts of sexual intimacy with patients during consultations would be a prosecution backed up by evidence of so high a degree of probative value that the public interest had priority over the risk of an unfair trial. Accordingly, the reception of the similar fact evidence was not erroneous.[77]

In the above passage, Heydon acknowledges that if one person says a psychiatrist abused her trust and convinced her to have sex with him, they might seem (to use the vernacular) a bit crazy. But if several patients say, 'He did it to me too,' the risk that all of them are crazy in the same way seems unlikely, and the case against the medico is strengthened.

The fact that, in 2011, Dyson Heydon offered up this prescient exposition of the reason why Me Too resonates with actual humans, is of more than passing interest. In his excellent article 'The Enemy Within', Jeremy Gans described it as startling that Heydon had 'used his judicial pulpit a decade ago to write something of a roadmap to his current predicament'. In light of the allegations concerning his conduct at the High Court, said Gans, Heydon's ruling on Stubley's appeal is 'a bit like Weinstein greenlighting a movie about a predatory producer'. As Gans went on to observe, Heydon may of course be innocent. On the other hand, 'he may have been somehow oblivious to his own conduct or supremely confident in his invulnerability, or maybe just intellectually devoted to his stance on evidence law. Each of these explanations,

RACHEL DOYLE

in different ways, suggest that Heydon may be his
own worst enemy.'[78]

Yes, indeed.

THE HEAVY BURDEN OF CIVIL LITIGATION

Civil remedies are individual and reactive. They are
only available in respect of specific instances of sexual
harassment which meet the tests in the legislation and
are found proven in accordance with the standard of
proof applied by the courts. Individual victims are
responsible for lodging complaints and prosecuting
their claims, a process which is expensive and may take
years to complete, and which imposes a substantial
burden on them.[79]

It is uncommon for multiple complainants to
jointly bring a single claim against a single alleged
sexual harasser.[80] There have been very few attempts
to test the application of the tendency evidence rules
in sexual harassment cases, and even fewer judicial
pronouncements upon the topic. The approaches
adopted by the courts to such attempts may explain
the reticence.

In 2010, a high-profile proceeding was launched
in the Federal Court against the retailer David Jones
and its then CEO, Mark McInnes. Kristy Fraser-Kirk,
a publicity coordinator, made allegations of sexual

harassment of a kind depressingly familiar to those who practise in the area: unwelcome sexual overtures, inappropriate touching, suggestive comments. The legal framework in which Fraser-Kirk sought to prosecute her claim possessed some novelty, relying on allegations of misleading and deceptive conduct under the *Trade Practices Act* and related claims of breach of contract and tort.[81] Fraser-Kirk alleged that David Jones, despite promoting its anti-harassment policies to staff internally, knew through senior management who had witnessed or had matters reported to them that McInnes had engaged in this sort of behaviour in the past, yet failed either to protect her or to respond appropriately when she raised concerns about him early on.

The pleadings alleged that there were a number of other employees of David Jones and Black & Decker (where McInnes had previously worked) who had also been subjected to various types of sexualised conduct by him. The allegations were outlined in the pleadings in brief terms, but the other targets of McInnes's conduct were not named. Early in the proceedings, an application was made by the defendants that the names be supplied to enable them to prepare a meaningful defence. The court ordered that this be done.[82] The case was resolved before the question of whether those other employees would or could give evidence was answered. It was reported in the press that David Jones and Fraser-Kirk settled the matter for $850 000.[83]

Had this trial run, it would have likely been a mini Me Too event. But as it was, there was no opportunity to see how the proposed tendency evidence might have changed the trajectory of the trial.

Three years later, a case concerning a woman employed by the Rivers clothing company came before the Federal Court: *Robinson v Goodman* [2013] FCA 893. The applicant alleged that while she was working at Rivers as a clothing designer, the company's owner, Philip Goodman, engaged in a calculated pattern of sexual pressure and harassment.[84] She applied to adduce tendency evidence from two former employees of the same company who said they had been subjected to many incidents of sexual harassment at the hands of Goodman. The other two women worked for the company prior to the applicant commencing there, and they had apparently never met each other.[85]

Justice Debra Mortimer concluded that just under half of the tendency evidence sought to be relied upon could be admitted.[86] Her Honour analysed at a granular level of detail the similarities between particular events and comments.[87] For example, she concluded that an incident during which Goodman was said to have touched a female employee's bottom was sufficiently similar to other allegations of bottom-touching to warrant admission into evidence. The same conclusion was reached in relation to an allegation of watching an employee model clothing, commenting on her breasts, and calling her 'Madam Lash'.[88] Other evidence was ruled inadmissible on the basis that it was insufficiently similar to the applicant's allegations.[89]

According to media reports, the Rivers case settled just hours after Justice Mortimer ruled that the evidence from the two women would be admitted into evidence.[90] We will never know why the case was settled, or why it was settled at that time. But one suspects it is no coincidence that the settlement came shortly after the ruling permitting the two employees to give evidence in support of the applicant.

There are some cases involving disciplinary proceedings against health professionals where a more robust approach to tendency evidence can be found.[91] But generally, attempts to rely upon tendency evidence in civil proceedings concerning sexual harassment have been remarkably few. One reason may be the timidity of practitioners. But I suspect the most significant problem is the difficulty attached to finding out whether there are other women who have been sexually harassed by the same perpetrator. If the alleged harasser has done it before, the statistical likelihood is that his behaviour has not been reported, much less litigated. Thus, one's capacity to locate potential witnesses is low.

Robinson v Goodman confirms the courts will search for a strong thread of commonality between the incidents. I argue that the degree of commonality for which the judges are searching is not required, and indeed is counterintuitive when one considers the way in which people typically act.

Assume the allegation in a civil proceeding concerning sexual harassment is that a male manager touched a female subordinate on the bottom when she was setting up a PowerPoint presentation. Assume the tendency evidence sought to be adduced is from two other female employees, who would (if permitted to give evidence) attest that they had also been touched by the manager while bending over to set up PowerPoint presentations. If, at trial, the man denies the complainant's allegation that he touched her, then one of the issues required to be determined by the trier of fact is whether the touching of her bottom happened at all. In that event, surely evidence from two others that something strikingly similar happened to them in the workplace is highly probative of whether it happened to her?

But let's tweak the example a little. What if one woman was alone with the manager because of a need to meet an important client late at night, and that is when he touched her backside? What if one woman's story is that just before other staff entered the lunch-room, he stared at her and said, 'I would love to touch your arse,' but he did not in fact do so. Why would those events not be relevant to proof of the question as to whether the alleged event had occurred, even though they are slightly different in their particulars?

I suggest that the courts should adopt a less-rigid approach to assessing tendency evidence in civil trials. In civil cases, there ought to be no requirement to demonstrate the existence of a precise modus operandi before material about the alleged harasser's past con-duct at work is probative. Surely the fact that a man has previously engaged in sexualised conduct with co-workers or subordinates is the point. This supplies the common thread the courts are looking for.

Fear not. I am not proposing that we start permit-ting a bloke's ex-wife to take to the stand and attest that he was a bit too handsy around the house. Nor do I suggest that we have a parade of Tinder users give evidence that the defendant told crude jokes on their first dates. Rather, what I propose is that the courts approach more flexibly the question of whether it is possible that evidence that a man has a history of making inappropriate sexualised comments, or of touching women at work, may be probative of an allegation of sexual harassment in the workplace.

COLLECTIVE RESPONSIBILITY

Bystander policies seek to convert workplace colleagues from mere observers to participants with a shared responsibility to ensure acts of sexual harassment are 'called out' at the time they happen. One of the recommendations made by the IBA in its *Us Too?* report was that the profession 'take ownership', which requires members

> to draw attention to inappropriate conduct when it happens and respond accordingly. For too long, the onus has been on the target to initiate a formal complaint before any action is contemplated. Bystanders must take a more prominent role in preventing and addressing bullying and sexual harassment—they can no longer be silent. To borrow a phrase from an entirely different context, 'if you see something, say something'.[92]

So far, so earnest. But what do you actually do if you witness sexual harassment?

Some very polite, if not wholly unrealistic, interventions are suggested in the AHRC's *Respect@Work* report, such as challenging the harasser by saying, 'What you said earlier really bothered me,' or, 'I wonder if you realise how that comes across?'[93] VicHealth also promotes active bystander policies. It suggests giving a 'disapproving look' or publicly declaring the action or statement of the perpetrator to be wrong or unacceptable.[94]

So how is this actually to be done, particularly in a professional environment? Imagine you are at a function attended by work colleagues and clients your employer needs to retain as well as potential clients your employer hopes to woo. The evening is going well. An impressive speech on a trending topic has been delivered by a manager. You find yourself in a small group, mostly sitting on mineral waters and eyeing their watches, thinking about how soon they will have to leave to relieve the babysitter. The group includes a man in his sixties who was a senior manager at the firm for many years and who, although officially retired, remains in the position of consultant. He is the reason some of the firm's most-important clients were recruited, and he continues to be the reason a number of them remain with the firm. He is drinking champagne and telling old war stories. You've heard them all before, but it's important to continue to smile and nod and keep the atmosphere pleasant. Indeed, others in the group who perhaps have not heard these stories seem to be enjoying themselves. At one point— and initially you convince yourself that this is just done for emphasis—he places his hand over the wrist of a young woman, very bright, very pretty, who is new to the firm. It seems like nothing. But a few minutes later, you see him shift his drink to his other hand. Then you see that while delivering the popular punchline to one of his stories, he has put his arm around the young woman and is now pulling her into his side quite aggressively. She is arching away from him, looking shocked and extremely uncomfortable.

'Well,' she says nervously, 'I should probably go and mingle.'

'Why?' he says, a little too loudly, a little too sharply. 'Will your boyfriend get jealous?'

'Well, no,' she mutters, embarrassed. 'I just don't want to take up any more of your time.'

'Oh, you can take up more of my time,' he says. 'In fact, you can take up my time anytime.'

The group falls quiet. The mood has shifted. Someone giggles nervously. The woman next to you looks furious. But no-one does anything.

What do you do? Meet her eye sympathetically and try to silently convey to her that you think he is being a dick? Do you try to smooth things over by saying something like, 'Come on mate, she's just doing what the firm asks us all to do, work the room!' Do you find a way to stand between her and him? Perhaps you could create a diversion by asking her if you can introduce her to a former client who has a project you are sure she might be interested in. All of these approaches might work, or none of them might. They might cause things to escalate, increase her embarrassment, or cause a scene.

Do you let things lie initially but go and speak to him alone later? Before doing so, do you check in with her? What if she says he ruined her night, but she just wants to stay quiet because she's scared of his influence in the firm? What if you do go to see him and he is dismissive, complains that you're laying it on a bit thick, that you have misinterpreted?

One thing is for sure, a decision to execute any one of these strategies calls for a degree of courage—and energy. Is it the case that at every function, all potential bystanders are 'on' with their moral certitude, and with their capacity to navigate treacherous waters locked and loaded? It is a big ask, I get it. But until we start to take responsibility by speaking up and calling out this behaviour, it is very unlikely things will change.

STONE COLD

When I first read Helen Garner's 1995 book *The First Stone*, it made me angry.[95] In it, Garner described her shocked reaction on reading that a university student had complained to the police about the master of Ormond College touching her breast at a college dance. Garner and her friends, whom she described as 'pushing fifty', could not believe the student had reported the master. Garner offered this stinging assessment: 'I thought I might be mad at these girls for not having *taken it like a woman*—for being wimps who ran to the law to whinge about a minor unpleasantness, instead of standing up and fighting back with their own weapons of youth and quick wits' [emphasis in the original]. Garner was vicious, referring to a 'literal-minded vengeance squad' and a 'certain kind of modern feminism: priggish, disingenuous, unforgiving'.[96]

There was a backlash against Garner in some quarters. My group of friends resolved not to give her any money by buying the book. Instead, we bought just one copy between us and circulated it among us. Each woman who read it made angry notations in the margins before passing it on to the next reader. We felt that 1970s feminists did not get it. They did not understand that now that the law had changed to render sexual harassment unlawful, and now that the police had been forced to be more victim-centric, surely young women could not be criticised for actually accessing the very laws Garner and her cabal of friends had championed when they were students.

But now that I am pushing fifty myself, just like Garner and her friends, I am experiencing my own revulsion at the new brand of feminism. Because of course in 2021, a young woman at law school who experiences a similar incident to that in *The First Stone* will be more likely to go straight home, open her laptop and 'cancel' the college master by using social media to spread her account of the night. And I would be horrified at that, just as Garner was horrified at what she regarded as the prudish and rigid response of the young women in her book.

Just as Garner criticised my generation for lacking the resilience to deal with the college master on the spot, I now find myself primly scolding millennials for indulging in lazy cancel-culture antics from the safety of their smartphones. And, in turn, those younger women tell me that I do not understand that social media is the new tool for exerting power, that it has taken over where all our fancy complaints procedures and nice sexual harassment training seminars have left off—or, more accurately, failed.

Millennials, can we meet in the middle? If I promise to educate men about what is unwelcome conduct in the workplace, if I undertake to change the system so that victims of recidivist sexual harassers can find each other and complain to management together, if I convince the courts to relax their rules for admitting evidence that a bloke at work has 'done it before', if I tackle the culture of silence and dismantle secret settlement deeds, if I educate your co-workers to call it out, then will you do something for me? Will you support each other, act collectively and confront harassers, but do it the way the six High Court associates did it? Go to the boss and tell your stories at the same time. Trust the process. Shut your laptops. Power down your phones. Work with us to build something new, rather than just chucking stones.

NOTES

1   See, for example, the *Equal Opportunity Act 2010* (Vic.), section
     92, and the *Anti Discrimination Act 1977* (NSW), section 22.

2   Susan Kiefel, 'Statement by the Hon Susan Kiefel AC, Chief Justice
     of the High Court of Australia', High Court of Australia, 22 June
     2020, https://cdn.hcourt.gov.au/assets/news/Statement%20
     by%20Chief%20Justice%20Susan%20Kiefel%20AC.pdf (viewed
     October 2020).

3   Rachel Doyle, 'The Word "Ashamed" Hit Me between the Eyes',
     The Age, 24 June 2020.

4   The article has been printed in a number of journals including
     Australian Bar Review ('Judicial Activism and the Death of the
     Rule of Law', vol. 23, 2003, pp. 110–33). As another example,
     in *Momcilovic v The Queen* (2011) 245 CLR 1, Heydon took a
     swipe at human rights lawyers, saying at [453] that 'the odour of
     human rights sanctity is sweet and addictive. It is a comforting
     drug stronger than poppy or mandragora or all the drowsy syrups
     of the world. But the effect can only be maintained over time by
     increasing the strength of the dose.'

5   See a partial transcript of the remarks on the ABC Radio National
     webpage: 'Heydon in His Own Words', 24 August 2015, https://
     www.abc.net.au/radionational/programs/archived/sundayprofile/
     dyson-heydon-in-his-own-words/6719864 (viewed October
     2020).

6   Michael Pelly, 'Judges' Union Pleads for End to "Unreasonable"
     Workloads', *The Sydney Morning Herald*, 11 October 2018.

7   Kate Eastman SC, 'Natural Justice Is a Golden Rule of
     Investigations. Has It Been Followed in the Heydon Case?' *The
     Guardian*, 24 June 2020.

8   Australian Human Rights Commission (AHRC), *Respect@Work:
     National Inquiry into Sexual Harassment in Australian Workplaces*,
     2020, p. 12.

9 Heydon was the NSW Rhodes scholar for 1964. He studied at University College, Oxford. By 1969, he was a lecturer at Oxford.

10 AHRC, *Everyone's Business: Fourth National Survey on Sexual Harassment in Australian Workplaces*, 2018, pp. 8, 26.

11 Ibid., p. 20.

12 AHRC, *Respect@Work*, p. 75; see also AHRC, *Everyone's Business*, p. 60.

13 AHRC, *Respect@Work*, p. 11.

14 See: Victorian Legal Services Board + Commissioner (VLSBC), *Sexual Harassment in the Victorian Legal Sector*, 2019. This study reported that 36 per cent of legal professionals had experienced sexual harassment: 61 per cent of women and 12 per cent of men. One in four legal professionals reported having experienced sexual harassment in the legal sector within the last twelve months, and 57 per cent within the last five years. See also: International Bar Association (IBA), *Us Too? Bullying and Sexual Harassment in the Legal Profession*, 2019. The IBA reported the results of a survey of 6980 respondents from 135 countries. Thirteen per cent of the respondents came from Australia. Of the respondents, 73 per cent came from law firms, 9 per cent from corporations or organisations, 5 per cent from government, 6 per cent from barristers' chambers and 3 per cent from the judiciary. One in three women and one in fourteen men reported having been sexually harassed in a work context. In Australia, 47 per cent of women working in the law experienced workplace sexual harassment, compared with 13 per cent of men. See also: *Victorian Bar, Quality of Working Life Survey: Final Report and Analysis*, October 2018. One in six women (16 per cent) and 2 per cent of men reported sexual harassment in the year preceding the survey, and in the previous five years, the reported rate for women went up to 25 per cent and down to 1 per cent for men.

15 AHRC, *Respect@Work*, p. 20; AHRC, *Everyone's Business*, p. 33.

16 Ibid., p. 33.

17 Ibid., p. 18.

18 AHRC, *Respect@Work*, p. 229; AHRC, *Everyone's Business*, pp. 44–5. See also: AHRC, *Respect@Work*, p. 201.

19 AHRC, *Everyone's Business*, pp. 38–9.

20   AHRC, *Respect@Work*, pp. 130–41, citing Afroditi Pina
and Theresa A Gannon, 'An Overview of the Literature on
Antecedents, Perceptions and Behavioural Consequences of
Sexual Harassment', *Journal of Sexual Aggression*, vol. 18, no. 2,
2012, pp. 209, 213, 214.

21   Elizabeth Shi and Freeman Zhong, 'Addressing Sexual Harassment
Law's Inadequacies in Altering Behaviour and Preventing Harm:
A Structural Approach', *UNSW Law Journal*, vol. 43, no. 1, 2020,
p. 155.

22   Pina and Gannon, 'An Overview of the Literature on Antecedents',
p. 214.

23   Male Champions of Change, *2019 Impact Report*, https://male
championsofchange.com/male-champions-of-change-release-the-
2019-combined-impact-report (viewed October 2020), p. 23.

24   AHRC, *Respect@Work*, pp. 78–9, 239.

25   Ibid., *Respect@Work*, p. 22. See also Deloitte, 'The Economic
Costs of Sexual Harassment in the Workplace', final report,
February 2019, pp. 5, 38–42, 75.

26   *Legal Services Commissioner v PLP* [2014] VCAT 793; *PLP v
McGarvie and VCAT* [2014] VSCA 253.

27   Ibid. [122]–[123].

28   *Lee v Smith & Ors* [2007] FMCA 59.

29   *B, C & D v Stratton* [1997] HREOCA 8.

30   *Tan v Xenos (No. 3)* (Anti-Discrimination) [2008] VCAT 584.

31   *Hughes Lawyers v Hill* [2020] FCAFC 126 at [11].

32   Ibid. at [40].

33   James Allsop, 'Public Statement from the Chief Justice', Federal
Court of Australia, 6 July 2020, https://www.fedcourt.gov.au/
news-and-events/6-july-2020-2 (viewed October 2020).

34   Cara Waters, 'Why a Bonk Ban Isn't Good for Business', *The
Sydney Morning Herald*, 16 February 2018; Josh Bornstein,
'Malcolm Turnbull's "Bonking Ban" Is a Misplaced Attack on
Consensual Sex', *The Sydney Morning Herald*, 17 February 2018.

35   AHRC, *Respect@Work*, p. 152; AHRC, *Everyone's Business*,
p. 67.

36   AHRC, *Everyone's Business*, pp. 10, 95.

37   AHRC, *Respect@Work*, pp. 15–16, 276.

38 VLSBC, *Sexual Harassment*, p. 52, fig. 24. The same report revealed this disconnect: 73 per cent of respondents to the Management Practices survey thought that sexual harassment was very rare within their own organisation, yet this report also revealed that 36 per cent of the profession said they had been sexually harassed: see p. 73, fig. 36.

39 IBA, *Us Too?*, p. 62, fig. 41.

40 Ibid., pp. 62–4.

41 AHRC, *Respect@Work*, p. 535.

42 Ibid., p. 32.

43 Ibid., pp. 609–10.

44 Ibid., p. 610 (referring to Unions NSW, Submission 354, *Sexual Harassment Inquiry*, p. 38).

45 AHRC, *Respect@Work*, p. 202.

46 Ibid., pp. 609–10.

47 Ibid., p. 604.

48 Ibid., p. 535.

49 IBA, *Us Too?*, p. 7.

50 Australian Solicitors' Conduct Rules and Legal Profession Uniform Conduct Rules.

51 In Victoria, an obligation is imposed by section 15 of the *Equal Opportunity Act 2020* to take reasonable and proportionate measures to eliminate sexual harassment. This section has not yet been tested, but it is unlikely to be interpreted as imposing a duty to report the conduct of others.

52 AHRC, *Respect@Work*, pp. 654, 668.

53 Ibid., 674.

54 Kate Eastman SC, 'Natural Justice Is a Golden Rule of Investigations. Has It Been Followed in the Heydon Case?', *The Guardian*, 24 June 2020.

55 AHRC, *Respect@Work*, pp. 653–4, 674.

56 The Vault application pioneered a feature called GoTogether, which enables the system to search for complaints against the same perpetrator and send them to management together (see http://www.vaultplatform.com). Callisto (https://mycallisto.org/detect-repeat-offenders) is used by some universities in the United States to enable students and staff to make a time-stamped

record of sexual harassment. When a complainant uses the 'Matching' function, the system holds the identity of the report writer in escrow until another victim of the same offender comes forward. See the discussion at AHRC, *Respect@Work*, pp. 665–7.

57 Stephen Gageler, 'Alternative Facts in the Courts', *Australian Law Journal*, vol. 93, 2019, p. 589.

58 Ibid., p. 593.

59 *Poniatowska v Hickinbotham* [2009] FCA 680, [47], [75].

60 Full disclaimer required: in the early stages of this litigation, I acted for one of the employing entities, which settled Ms Vergara's claim against it. Nothing I say here draws on information I gained in that proceeding. It is solely derived from the reasons of the Federal Court, which are public.

61 *Ewin v Vergara (No. 3)* [2013] FCA 1311, [45]–[46].

62 *Evidence Act 2005* (Cth), sections 97, 101.

63 See *HML v The Queen* (2008) 235 CLR 334, *IMM v The Queen* (2016) 257 CLR 300, *Hughes v The Queen* (2017) 92 ALJR 52 and *Queen v Dennis Bauer* (2018) 92 ALJR 846, [48]–[58]. *Bauer* was a single judgment handed down by seven judges in mid-September 2019.

64 Five judges sat on *McPhillamy* (2018) 361 ALR 13 (Kiefel CJ and justices Bell, Keane, Nettle and Edelman). The decision was only three months after seven judges had decided *Bauer*.

65 *McPhillamy*, [26].

66 Ibid., [26]–[27], [31]–[32], [36]–[38].

67 *Hughes*, [70] (Gageler J, dissenting).

68 Ibid., [200] (Nettle J, dissenting).

69 Ibid., [109] (Gageler J, dissenting).

70 Annie Cossins, 'The Future of Joint Trials of Sex Offences after Hughes: Resolving Judicial Fears and Jurisdictional Tensions with Evidence-Based Decision-Making', *Melbourne University Law Review*, vol. 41, no. 3, 2018, p. 1121.

71 Ibid., referring to the 2016 study presented to the Royal Commission into Institutional Responses to Child Sexual Abuse: Jane Goodman-Delahunty, Annie Cossins and Natalie Martschuk, *Jury Reasoning in Joint and Separate Trials of Institutional Child*

Sexual Abuse: An Empirical Study, Commonwealth Government, Sydney, 2016.

72   *Stubley v Western Australia* (2011) 85 ALJR 435.

73   Ibid., [56].

74   Ibid., [102].

75   Ibid., [73].

76   Ibid., [87].

77   Ibid., [143].

78   Jeremy Gans, 'The Enemy Within', *Inside Story*, 26 June 2020. The title of the Gans article comes from a speech Heydon gave in January 2012 at Oxford University titled, 'Threats to Judicial Independence: The Enemy Within'.

79   Shi and Zhong, 'Addressing Sexual Harassment Law's Inadequacies'.

80   See, for example: *B, C & D v Stratton* [1997] HREOCA 8 (three women employed in administrative roles in the same workplace); and *Romari-Whittle & Ors v Godfrey & Ors* [2000] VCAT 1847 (four female security guards working at the same site and alleging sex discrimination and sexual harassment).

81   More standard allegations of sexual harassment were also made under the *Sex Discrimination Act* in a separate claim to the AHRC.

82   *Fraser-Kirk v David Jones Limited* [2010] FCA 1060.

83   Fenella Souter, 'The Damage Done', *The Sydney Morning Herald*, 28 August 2014.

84   *Robinson v Goodman* [2013] FCA 893, [29].

85   Emily Portelli, 'Rivers Boss Philip Goodman Settles Sexual Harassment Case', *Herald Sun*, 2 September 2013.

86   *Robinson v Goodman* [2013] FCA 893, [35].

87   Ibid., [36]–[51].

88   Ibid., [35].

89   Ibid., [51].

90   Emily Portelli, 'Rivers Boss Philip Goodman Settles Sexual Harassment Case', *Herald Sun*, 2 September 2013.

91   *Nursing and Midwifery Board of Australia v Singh (Review and Regulation)* [2014] VCAT 1171; on appeal: *Singh v Nursing and Midwifery Board of Australia* [2015] VSC 576. There, the

tribunal expressly adopted the approach used in *Robinson v Goodman* [2013] FCA 893. See also *Purnell v Medical Board of Queensland* [1999] 1 QdR 362; *Medical Board of Australia v Gomez* [2015] QCAT 121; and *Medical Board of Australia v Lee* [2019] VCAT 2036.

92   IBA, *Us Too?*, p. 103.

93   AHRC, *Respect@Work*, pp. 724–5, referring to the submissions of the Diversity Council Australia, National Workplace *Sexual Harassment Inquiry,* submission 282, pp. 7, 43.

94   VicHealth, 'Take Action: Empowering Bystanders to Act on Sexist and Sexually Harassing Behaviours in Universities', 2019, p. 3.

95   Helen Garner, *The First Stone: Some Questions about Sex and Power*, Picador, Sydney, 1995.

96   Ibid., pp. 40, 93, 202.